GEORGE FRIDERIC HANDEL

WATER MUSIC

Edited by/Herausgegeben von/Édition de
Roger Fiske

Ernst Eulenburg Ltd

London · Mainz · Madrid · New York · Paris · Tokyo · Toronto · Zürich

CONTENTS

Suite No. 3 in G

Performance material based on this edition is available from the publisher/
Der hier veröffentlichte Notentext ist auch als Aufführungsmaterial beim Verlag erhältlich/
Le matériel d'exécution réalisé à partir de cette édition est disponible auprès de l'éditeur

Eulenburg Orchestral Series: EOS 1308

Ernst Eulenburg Ltd
48 Great Marlborough Street
London W1F 7BB

PREFACE

On 19 July 1717 the *Daily Courant* reported an event that had taken place two days earlier:

'On Wednesday Evening, at about 8, the King took Water at Whitehall in an open Barge [...] and went up the River towards Chelsea. Many other Barges with Persons of Quality attended [...] A City Company's Barge was employ'd for the Musick, wherein were 50 Instruments of all sorts, who play'd all the way from Lambeth (while the Barges drove with the Tide without rowing, as far as Chelsea) the finest Symphonies, compos'd express for this Occasion, by Mr. Hendel; which his Majesty liked so well, that he caus'd it to be plaid over three times in going and returning. At Eleven his Majesty went a-shore at Chelsea, where a Supper was prepar'd, and then there was another very fine Consort of Musick, which lasted till 2; after which, his Majesty came again into his Barge, and return'd the same way, the Musick continuing to play till he landed.'

In a private report, Friedrich Bonet, the Prussian Resident in London, added the information that the instruments on the barge included trumpets, horns, oboes, bassoons, German flutes, recorders and strings; and that each performance lasted an hour; that there were two performances before supper and one after; and that the orchestra cost £150, and was paid for by Baron Kielmansegge. (The Baron's wife, Madame Keilmansegge, was George I's rather elderly mistress.)

Handel's first biographer, John Mainwaring, has an anecdote about a water party of 1715 for which Handel composed music, and though the details of his account are now discredited, it is likely that an earlier water party did take place. There were many such occasions later in the century. In a letter of 14 July 1722 (quoted in her autobiography), Mrs Delany described a night when barges were rowed upstream from Whitehall Stairs to Richmond, and 'the concert was composed of three hautboys, two bassoons, flute allemagne, and young Grenoc's trumpet'. Such a combination can hardly have played Handel's *Water Music*, but when spurious pieces were published as coming from this work, they may well have been written for rival river picnics that were no concern of Handel's.

The autograph of the *Water Music* vanished in the 18th century (ruined by wind and water?), and the music was never adequately published in Handel's lifetime. This had led to more editorial despair than the situation warrants, most of it inherited from Chrysander. In spite of what has been averred to the contrary, the music survives in good MSS that agree reasonably well with each other, all of it fully scored and in a sensible order.

The printed sources, however, are unhelpful, and I have made but little use of them. The more important are listed below in chronological order, and for some of the information I have drawn on William C. Smith's *Handel, A Descriptive Catalogue* (London, 1960). Pieces are identified by the editorial numbering in this study score. Self-explanatory abbreviations to the left of the sources are used later in the Editorial Notes. PP means Printed Parts.

Arrangements of minuets: 6 and 12 for harpsichord in *The Lady's Banquet* III (1720; only the c.1732 edition seems to survive); 6 as

'Phillis the lovely' and 'Thirsis, afflicted with Love' (c.1725), and in ballad operas (e.g. Air 19 in Gay's Polly of 1729); 12 as 'When I beheld Clarinda's Eyes' and 'Hark, how the Trumpet sounds' (c.1720), and in ballad operas (e.g. Air 28 in both *Polly* and *Momus turn'd Fabulist*); 17 as 'Lovely Cloe' (c.1725, and in *The Musical Miscellany* V). 6 and 12 are usually called 'Minuet for the French Horn' and 'Trumpet Minuet' without reference to the *Water Music*. Basses, if any, are not Handel's.

PP/Ov: *Six Overtures for Violins in all their Parts*, Walsh's third Collection, includes the 'Water Music' Overture among Handel opera overtures; Smith gives c.1725, but the BL parts (incomplete) include *Admeto* and cannot be before 1727. The *Water Music* overture is also in later and larger collections of Handel overtures. All these editions are basically the same. The eight parts are: *Hautboy, Violino Primo, Violino Secondo, Violino Primo Ripieno, Violino Secondo Ripieno, Tenor, Bassoon e Violoncello, Basso Continuo*.

PP: *The Celebrated Water Musick in seven Parts* (1733) includes 3, 4, 8–9, 10D, 11D, 13–16 in that order. This suggests that Walsh selected from a source in the order I have accepted, the 1717 autograph no doubt. Orchestras in the playhouses and elsewhere seldom included trumpets, so Walsh incorporated the trumpet notes in the horn parts, altering the latter where necessary. He issued one part for Violin I and Oboe 1, another for Violin II and Oboe 2; sometimes the engraver managed to get both instrumental lines onto one stave, but mostly he omitted whichever seemed the less important. In 9

the result is chaotic. Yet these parts (2 horns, bassoon, strings) were constantly played all over Britain, for instance as interval music in the London theatres; sometimes kettledrums were advertised as a special attraction, but no parts survive. It is odd that Walsh left out the already popular minuets.

Hps: *Handel's Celebrated Water Musick compleat. Set for the Harpsichord* (1743) omits No. 9, but includes all the other pieces in the order I have accepted. Some were not available in any other form during Handel's lifetime. By 1743 Handel may have abstracted 9 with a view to including it in some other work; or perhaps it was mislaid or damaged by a copyist.

Arn: Samuel Arnold's 'Complete Works' edition (1788); the first published full score.

HG: Händelgesellschaft, Vol. 47 edited by Friedrich Chrysander; Chrysander based his edition on Arnold, the only full score he ever saw.

The Famous Water Peice published in parts by Wright (1733) is surely spurious. The 'Overture' looks like a pirated version of 10D, written down from memory; Nos. 2 and 3 are not known to be by Handel, and 3 could not be played without a harpsichord. All five pieces are naively scored for trumpet and strings. No. 5 had appeared in *Partenope* (1730).

Manuscript sources:

AUT: *GB-Lbl* Add. 30310 contains 10F and 11F in Handel's autograph (1715? See below).

Gran: *GB-Lbl* Egerton 2946 is from the Granville Collection of 'library' scores copied for Bernard Granville, Handel's friend and Mrs Delany's brother. The collection remained in the family until 1915. This carefully written MS cannot be earlier than 1736 because it contains the 'Alexander's Feast' Concerto, nor later than 1743 because it includes 9, the piece not available for Hps. The most reliable source.

BL: Fitzwilliam Music *GB-Cfm* MS 836 (BL 67) at Cambridge is from the Barrett Lennard Collection bought in 1902. Another 'library' copy made by the elder J.C.Smith or one of his staff. As it omits No. 9, it must be later than Gran.

Ayles: Manchester Public Library has a score and a set of parts copied by Smith or his staff for Handel's librettist, Charles Jennens, who must have planned to perform the music. His important MS collection passed to the Earl of Aylesford, and in 1918 the Aylesford Collection was bought by Newman Flower. At Flower's death it went to Manchester. The score is on 10-stave paper that sometimes left the copyist no space for the bassoon part (e.g. in 13). There are far more mistakes than in Gran or BL, but as the parts agree well with the score the copyist must have had an inferior source. The many errors are not listed below, but see 6 (bb52–54) and 18 (bb15–22) where he cooked up his own bass, making most of it double the viola; perhaps the bass stave in his source had been torn off at the foot of a page. The flute parts were given in the oboe parts so that they could be played by the oboists. The 14 partbooks are: Hautboy I and II, Corno I and II, Tromba I and II, Violino Concertino I and II, Violino 'Ripieno' I and II, Viola, Violoncello, Contra Basso, 'Basson'. The order of the pieces is not that of Gran, BL and Hps. Ayles includes 9 and may be earlier than BL and before 1743.

It was long ago suggested, and by the 1950s it was accepted, that the *Water Music* is an amalgam of at least two suites. This, however, was denied by Chrysander, even though he came upon evidence for it. It was he who advised the British Museum to buy the two movements in Handel's autograph, 10F and 11F, and he published them on their own as a 'Concerto'. They are early versions of 10D and 11D (my enumeration distinguishes them by key), and in this study score they are for the first time restored to their proper place at the end of the first suite.

We can now build up a picture of how all this music came to be assembled in the various sources. For the first water party (1715?) Handel wrote a suite in F, and because it was outdoor music he made use, for virtually the first time in England, of French horns; the players probably came from Bohemia, as did Bach's horn players. When the 1717 water party was suggested Handel decided to include trumpets, the most effective of all instruments out-of-doors, and because English trumpeters almost always played in D he had to compose the new music in that key. He repeated his earlier suite, both to fill the playing time with a minimum of effort and perhaps also because there had been a request for it, but he did not wish to delay for too long the entry of the trumpets. He may well have remembered that the dynamic contrasts in 10F and the violin writing in the middle section had been ineffective out-of-doors, so he completely rewrote this movement in a more robust style, and put both this and 11F into D so that he could add trumpets to the scoring. In their original form these movements were redundant, so Handel detached them from the autograph and they chanced to survive. He added three new pieces for full band, and was so eager for a grand effect that he allowed himself no dynamic contrasts in the D major suite; the five pieces were to be performed *fortissimo* throughout.

Movements 15–19 are in yet another key, G, and feature the two main kinds of flute. They are so quietly scored that they can hardly have been intended as river music. Almost certainly they were the 'very fine Consort of Musick' performed while the King had supper at Chelsea. The Prussian Resident mentioned both kinds of flute as being played on the barge; if they were played in the outdoor music, they must have doubled the oboe parts.

Gran, BL, and Hps all give the music in what I believe was the 1717 order. I have preserved that order here. The titles of the suites are, of course, editorial:

I Suite No.1 in F p.1
II Suite No.2 in D p.67
III Suite No.3 in G p.88

This order was acceptable for 'library' MSS, but not for anyone like Jennens who wanted to perform the music as a single work. Somebody, and just possibly it was Handel, devised a different order, perhaps in the first instance for later water parties, mixing the second and third suites to achieve more contrast and a rousing end. Ayles derived from such a score, and gave the pieces thus:

1–5, 7–8, 6, 9, 10D, 11D, 15–16, 13–14, 17–19, 12

Arn and HG followed this order except that they put 6 between 5 and 7. Arnold knew of the original order, but preferred to print the work as though it were a single whole.

There is nothing to prevent those who use this score and the parts that go with it from adopting Arnold's order, or any other of their own devising. Obviously this edition should not be played straight through unless the Trumpet Suite is repeated at the end; Handel repeated *both* the earlier suites at the end. In such performances, 10F and 11F must be omitted. Any of the suites can be played on its own, and the first would be especially effective; or the Horn and Trumpet Suites can be played consecutively (without 10F and 11F), as indeed they were on the Thames in 1717.

Editorial Notes

In the main I have followed Gran and BL which are very accurate and very similar to each other. I believe they were copied from the autograph, whereas Ayles was copied from a less accurate score. I have taken titles, tempo marks, etc., from any source that gives them, such details being in short supply. When not mentioned below, they are in Gran and BL. 'Tempo in BL' implies that there is no tempo mark in other sources.

There can hardly have been a harpsichord on the barge. Handel made sure that all the music was harmonically complete, and had no reason to figure the bass. Gran has no figures, BL only in the first part of 5 and in 17. PP/Ov, PP and Ayles are fully figured, but the figures bear little resemblance to each other, those in PP being very inaccurate. A concordance would take pages and interest no one. It is so unlikely that any surviving figures are Handel's that I have preferred to give none at all. Arnold's are sensible and can be found in HG.

The horn parts present a problem. In Suite 1 Gran, BL and (for the most part) Ayles give them in the usual way – visually in C with no key signature. But in the Trumpet Suite Gran, BL, and Ayles (Full Score) give all the brass *loco* with a 2-sharp key signature. English trumpet parts were nearly always so written, and normally were by Handel. In Nos. 12 and 14 he must have saved himself trouble by making his horns double the trumpets on the same staves, for the parts were so copied in Gran and BL. But key signatures were very unusual in horn parts, and the Ayles copyist did not accept them; throughout the Trumpet Suite he transposed the horn parts into C. PP has transposing horn parts, and I have preferred this convention too. I hope it will not seem inconsistent that the trumpet parts have been left *loco* with a key signature.

'Bassons' in the plural is common in Gran and BL, but the part never divides, and it is not clear whether two or more were expected.

Rubrics: in what follows, 'b45, VIII, n7' means 'bar 45, Second Violin stave, seventh note'.

Editorial markings: editorial additions are placed within square brackets; editorial slurs or ties are shown as broken lines.

Suite 1

1. b1: Largo, PP/Ov. Besides the 'Hautboy Solo' part, Walsh reproduced among the Ob2 parts of the other overtures the VIrip.II part of this one. Thus Handel presumably wanted Ob2 to double VIrip.II, which it does in Ayles and in this score. The same sources indicate Fg doubling Vc throughout. Gran and BL show Largo on 4 unidentified staves, which probably imply woodwind doubling.
   b2, VII/Ob1, n1. The only *tr* in MS sources of the Largo. All the subsequently bracketted *tr* are from Hps. Another might be added in b1, beat 3.
   b27, Ob1, 'Solo' in Gran, BL, and Ayles; cancelled by 'Tutti' in b34. This shows that elsewhere the part was played by at least 2 players. No source has 'Solo' at b40.

b44, VIII, n7. HG alone has natural; Gran and HG have repeated quavers on 4th beat in VIconc.I, but BL's crotchet seems better.

b55, VI rip.I, nn 7–8. Gran, BL, Arn/HG show notes reversed (Arn/HG Ob1 as well); I have made them conform with the fugue subject.

b76. Only PP/Ov gives 2nd ending (with Ob1 senselessly doubling VIconc.I at b77). There is nothing to show the start of the repeat.

2. VIconc. staves in Gran, BL, Ayles, Arn, but they double VIrip.I & II. Ob2 pointlessly doubles VIII in Ayles, and Fg doubles Basso; Fg doubling is implied in Gran and BL. Fg alone might play 16–18. Ob1 should decorate.

bb18–20: corrupt. In b20 Gran, BL have crotchets for Vla that do not fit; I have moved them to b19 and invented notes for b20. In b18 Gran and Arn/HG have improbable crotchets for VII on beats 2 and 3 (BL a third higher), but Ayles *forte* in b19 confirms that b19 is the entry; also VII conc. has a bar's rest in b18, so VIrip.I should too, for the parts are identical. I give the 2 crotchets to Vla, which now has a sensible part. (Arn and all modern editions give the Vla rests in bb18–20, but b21 is impossibe as an entry.)

3. Allegro, Ayles, Hps.

bb3, 5, 7: Fg & Vla *tr* Gran, Ayles. In b2 PP, BL, Arn have *tr* for Cor 2.

bb50–53: confusion between ♫ and ♩♪. HG has only A, PP only B, other sources a mixture. If we presume an error at b51, an alternative pattern emerges in Gran, BL, and Ayles, and this is given here.

b106: theme from Oboe Sonata Op1/6, which gives *tr* on n6. Gran, BL,

Ayles give similar *tr* at b126, and I have added others in brackets; all those in bb106–119 are from Hps.

4. Presto. Ayles.
Two identical Ob staves in Gran & BL. Ayles has Ob2 doubling VIII, which puts the entire part above Ob1.

b3: Cor 2, n2. All sources give e′, but it can hardly be right.

b5: confusion between ♫♩ and ♩♫. All sources differ, and no pattern emerges. One or other must be chosen. I give B because it predominates, but all sources have A at b13 (except Hps).

b39: Vla, n3. HG gives incorrect B′♭; Arn's note could be either B′♭ or c″.

bb47–81: all sources have Fg doubling Basso except Ayles FS, which gives rests.

b64: VIII, n2: HG has unnecessary natural, which all later editions follow.

bb67–73: Handel's dots and quaver rests may need rationalising.

5. Presto, Ayles, FS and Parts (!). '3 Fois' Arn/HG only. Ayles has Obs doubling Vlns, and Fg doubling Basso throughout, but Gran shows no woodwind. BL has 'Tutti Hautb' at b19 on VII stave, which Arn accepted and so do I. It seems reasonable to add Fg from b19. There is no authority for a *pp Da Capo* for strings alone.

b25: undotted in Ayles and Arn/HG, in error; VII dotted in Gran and BL, and Cor 2 should probably be dotted too. Perhaps also Fg, VIII and Basso.

6. Title from song arrangements. '3 Fois' Arn/HG only. I have found no authority for the 16-bar introduction for horns alone in Arn/HG.

b17: for tunes in the tenor register with

Vl accompanying above, see 3 (bb56–60), 19 (bb9–16), and the trio of the minuet in Op3/4. Early sources have a 3-flat key signature which I have adjusted.

b31: Fg, Vla, n6 a♭ in Arn and all editions since; Handel wanted f, but VIII could not play it.

7. Presto, Ayles, which alone has barred C. '3 times […] altogether' Gran, BL (not Ayles). As in No. 8, Gran, BL have 4 staves; Ayles FS has 8.

8. '3 times […] manner', Gran, BL.

9. Not in BL or Hps; very corruptly in PP.

b25: Ob2, n7. Gran ♮, so I have added ♮s at start of b26. Arn, HG give these notes as b♭.

b34: Fg, Basso, n11. F in PP and Ayles.

10F. b3: Ob1, n4. HG f″; Handel wrote both this note and c″.

b34: VII, n7. HG c″, which Handel wrote first but then altered.

11F. cf Flute Sonata, Op1/9, mvt 2.

b23: Ob2, Vla, n4. HG added unnecessary ♭.

Suite 2

10D. Allegro, Ayles. BL has stave for 'Bassons', PP and Ayles a Fg part; Gran and Ayles FS has no room for a stave, and had to omit individual notes in bb8–9, 15, 22, 35. Hps alone has dynamics: *p* for Cor tunes and *f* for Tr tunes, but the reverse in bb9–11. Hps adds a in Bass on last quaver of b5 (cf next bar), and decorates slightly in bb6–7, 12–14, etc.

b20: omitted in BL at a page-turn.

bb48–50: given in PP, Gran, BL, Arn; not in Hps or Ayles.

b50: VII, n1, *tr* in Gran. VIII, n1, *tr* in Gran, BL. HG has VIII wrongly.

11D. Gran, BL have 2 violin staves to b39, and then 3. Fg stave as in 10D, but b11: dotted semibreves need shortening. Tr2, bb11–14 chaotic in Ayles.

b40: VII in Ayles marked 'Violino Concertino'.

b64: Ob1, 2, bb2–3. Gran, BL, Ayles, Arn have instead crotchet f♯.

b69: VIII, nn6–7. As in Gran, BL; Arn/HG have crotchet d♯ for the quavers.

b74: No *Da Capo* in Gran, BL, but one is implied by pauses at b39, and given in Ayles and Arn/HG.

12. 'Trumpet Minuet' in early song arrangements and literary references; 'Menuet' Gran, BL; 'Coro' in Arn. '3 times […] together' Gran, BL (not Ayles); Gran and BL give 3 violin staves, Ayles 2.

bb4, 6: *tr* in 1st beat Hps only.

14. 'This Aire […]thrice', PP VII; similarly other PP and HG, but not Gran, BL, Ayles or Arn. It surely was and should be repeated as No. 12.

Suite 3

15. 'Travers e Viol.I' on same stave, Gran, BL; they can alternate at repeats. Hps has *tr* bb7, 27, 43; all sources bb31, 33; only Arn/HG in bb1, 3 (on d″).

16. Presto, Ayles. 'Aria', Arn/HG. 4 staves Gran, BL, Arn, perhaps for strings alone, but Ayles copyist thought top stave was for 'Travers' as in 15, and had all Vlns on 2nd stave and Fg doubling Basso on 4th. PP carelessly showed Obs doubling Vlns as earlier, and this was followed by HG even though it takes Ob2 out of its compass.

b38: apparently a separate piece in Gran, BL; PP gives it a separate number. But it has no time signature, and strongly resembles bb1–37 in rhythm.

Gran's 'senza fag.' in Basso at b66 implies Fg doubling earlier.

Ayles implies a *Da Capo* with pauses at b37, and Arn/HG follow doubtfully; as I do. Ayles has unbarred C at b38, and 'Hoboe I & II, Viola, Fagotto' on the 4 staves, which would be attractive. Early sources have a 1-flat key signature, which I have adjusted.

b42: Basso, 4. c′ in BL, Hps; VIII, 4, would then be a′ or e″♭, but all sources give d″.

17. 'Menuet', Gran, BL. 'Twice', Gran. BL implies strings only. Ayles has Fg doubling Basso, and this may be implied by Gran's 'Tutti' on Basso stave. Arn/HG have 2 Fg and Vc on bottom stave, without Cb.

b9: Vla, n2, c′ in Arn/HG is wrong.

bb15, 16: Vl slurred on 1st beat BL.

18. 'Flauto piccoli', Gran, BL; 'Flautino', Ayles. The part shows that descant recorders are required. All sources give the part a 4th above Vl, meaning it to sound a 5th higher still, and with a 3-flat key signature. For modern performance I give the notes an octave below sounding pitch with a 2-flat key signature. 'Twice', Gran, referring perhaps to the *Da Capo*.

19. 'Country Dance Alternativement, twice', Gran. I give Gran's string parts but BL, Ayles, Arn/HG have VIII playing Gran's Vla, and Vla doubling Vc. The intention seems to have been to contrast an unusually emphasized high tune with an unusually emphasized low one, but not certainly in *Da Capo* form. No source has *Da Capo* or pauses in b8; all but HG give unbarred C for the G minor dance, and barred C for the G major, which may imply different tempos. In favour of *Da Capo* form are Gran's title and 'Volti subito' after b8, and the obvious similarity of style. Slurs

and triplet 3s are as in Ayles, but the slurs may indicate triplets rather than bowing and as such they can be ignored.

b13: Basso, nn2–3. Even quavers in all sources, but Handel must have meant to dot the c. Perhaps the Vlas even quavers in bb7, 8 should be dotted too.

b14: VlI, n11. As in Gran. BL, Ayles, Arn/HG have c″

Instrumentation

I. [Horn Suite]
2 Oboes (4 players?)
1 Bassoon (2 players?)
2 Horns (4 players?)
Strings

II. [Trumpet Suite]
2 Oboes (4 players?)
1 Bassoon (2 players?)
2 Horns (4 players?)
2 Trumpets (4 players?)
Strings

III. [Flute Suite]
2 descant recorders (one doubling flute)
1 Bassoon
Strings
Harpsichord

In 1717 Handel had '50 Instruments of all sorts'; the wind parts were certainly doubled, and if possible they should be doubled today.

In the Flute Suite the strings should be reduced, and a harpsichord should be added. In the other suites the harpsichord is optional.

Roger Fiske
(1973)

VORWORT

Der *Daily Courant* vom 19. Juli 1717 berichtete von einem Ereignis, das sich zwei Tage zuvor zugetragen hatte, wie folgt:

„Am Mittwochabend, ungefähr um acht Uhr, begab sich der König in einem offenen Schiff auf eine Bootsfahrt [...] und fuhr flussaufwärts nach Chelsea. Er wurde von vielen anderen Booten begleitet, die mit Personen von Rang und Namen besetzt waren. Auf einem der Schiffe befanden sich die Musiker, die über 50 Instrumente jeglicher Art verfügten. Sie spielten die ganze Zeit ab Lambeth (während die Boote von der Strömung getrieben und bis Chelsea nicht gerudert werden mussten) die schönsten Sinfonien, die Händel extra für diesen Anlass komponiert hatte. Sie gefielen Seiner Majestät derart, dass sie auf der Hin- und Rückfahrt dreimal wiederholt werden mussten. Um elf Uhr ging Seine Majestät in Chelsea an Land, wo ihn ein Souper erwartete. Auch hier wurde wieder sehr schöne Musik gespielt, die bis zwei Uhr andauerte. Danach bestieg Seine Majestät wieder das Schiff und fuhr denselben Weg zurück, wobei weiterhin musiziert wurde, bis der König an Land ging."

In einem persönlichen Bericht fügte Friedrich Bonet, Preußischer Gesandter in London, außerdem hinzu, dass das auf dem Schiff befindliche Orchester aus Trompeten, Hörnern, Oboen, Fagotten, Querflöten, Blockflöten und Streichern bestand, dass die Aufführung des ganzen Werks jeweils eine Stunde lang dauerte und dass zwei Aufführungen vor und eine nach dem Souper stattgefunden hat. Die Kosten für das Orchester in Höhe von £ 150 sollen von Baron Kielmansegge übernommen worden sein. (Die Frau des Barons, Madame Kielmansegge, war trotz ihres vorgeschrittenen Alters die Mätresse von Georg I.)

John Mainwaring, dem wir die erste Händel-Biografie verdanken, erwähnt eine Lustfahrt auf dem Wasser aus dem Jahre 1715, für die Händel die Musik geschrieben haben soll. Obgleich sein Bericht heute nicht mehr in jeder Hinsicht glaubwürdig erscheint, ist doch anzunehmen, dass eine solche Lustfahrt zu einem früheren Datum stattgefunden hat. Belustigungen dieser Art fanden jedenfalls im weiteren Verlauf des Jahrhunderts häufiger statt. Mrs Delany zitiert in ihrer Autobiografie einen Brief vom 14. Juli 1722, in dem sie einen Abend beschreibt, an welchem Boote flussaufwärts von Whitehall Stairs nach Richmond gerudert wurden, wobei „die Musik aus drei Oboen, zwei Fagotten, Querflöte und der Trompete des jungen Grenoc bestand". Eine solche Besetzung wäre kaum in der Lage gewesen, Händels *Wassermusik* zu spielen. Es ist aber durchaus möglich, dass Stücke zu anderen Lustfahrten entstanden sind, die als angebliche Werke Händels veröffentlicht wurden, obwohl sie mit Händels Musik nichts zu tun hatten.

Das Autograph der *Wassermusik* kam schon im 18. Jahrhundert abhanden (vielleicht vom Wind und Wasser zerstört?), und das Werk ist zu Händels Lebzeiten nie in einer brauchbaren Form veröffentlicht worden. Die dadurch entstandene Verzweiflung späterer Herausgeber, für die Chrysander größtenteils verantwortlich ist, erscheint jedoch nicht ganz gerechtfertigt. Trotz aller gegenteiligen Behauptungen blieb die Komposition nämlich in einer

Reihe recht gut übereinstimmender Manuskripte erhalten, die durchgehend instrumentiert sind und die Stücke in einer sinngemäßen Reihenfolge wiedergeben.

Die ersten gedruckten Quellen sind allerdings nicht sehr aufschlussreich; daher habe ich davon nur wenig Gebrauch gemacht. Die wichtigsten unter ihnen sind weiter unten in chronologischer Reihenfolge aufgeführt. Ich habe mich dabei zum Teil auf C. Smiths Werk *Handel, A Descriptive Catalogue* (London, 1960) berufen. Die einzelnen Stücke sind durch die in der vorliegenden Taschenpartitur verwandte Nummerierung bezeichnet. Klar verständliche Abkürzungen, die links von den angegebenen Quellen stehen, werden auch in den folgenden Anmerkungen des Herausgebers verwandt. PP bedeutet gedruckte Stimmen [Printed Parts].

Arrangements von Menuetten: Nr. 6 und Nr. 12 für Cembalo arrangiert in *The Lady's Banquet III* (1720; nur die Ausgabe von ca. 1732 scheint erhalten); Nr. 6 arrangiert als *Phillis the lovely* und *Thirsis, afflicted with Love* (ca. 1725) und in den „ballad operas" genannten Singspielen (z. B. Arie Nr. 19 in *Polly*, einer Oper von Gay aus dem Jahre 1729); Nr. 12 arrangiert als *When I beheld Clarinda's Eyes* und *Hark, how the Trumpet sounds* (ca. 1720) sowie in Singspielen (z. B. Arie Nr. 28, sowohl in *Polly* als auch in *Momus turn'd Fabulist*); Nr. 17 arrangiert als *Lovely Cloe* (ca. 1725 und in *The Musical Miscellany V*); Nr. 6 und Nr. 12 sind als *Minuet for the French Horn* und *Trumpet Minuet* bekannt, aber nicht in Zusammenhang mit der *Wassermusik*. Die Bassstimmen, soweit angegeben, stammen nicht von Händel.

PP/Ov: *Six Overtures for Violins in all their Parts*, 3. Sammlung von Walsh. In diesem Band findet man die Ouvertüre der *Wassermusik* unter Händels Opernouvertüren. Smith gibt als Entstehungsjahr ca. 1725 an. Da aber die (unvollständigen) Stimmen von *Admeto* in der British Library zu finden sind, kann frühestens 1727 als Datum angenommen werden. Die Ouvertüre der *Wassermusik* erscheint auch in späteren und größeren Sammlungen mit Ouvertüren von Händel, die im Großen und Ganzen übereinstimmen. Die angegebenen acht Stimmen wurden wie folgt bezeichnet: „Hautboy, Violino Primo, Violino Secondo, Violino Primo Ripieno, Violino Secondo Ripieno, Tenor, Bassoon e Violoncello, Basso Continuo".

PP: *The Celebrated Water Musick in seven Parts* (1733), bestehend aus den Nummern 3, 4, 8–9, 10D, 11D und 13–16 in dieser Reihenfolge. Daraus wäre zu schließen, dass Walsh seine Auswahl nach einer Vorlage getroffen hat, die mit der von mir gewählten Reihenfolge übereinstimmt; vermutlich das Manuskript von 1717. Da Theaterorchester und andere Orchester damals selten über Trompeten verfügten, arbeitete Walsh die Trompetennoten in die Hornstimmen mit ein, die er, wenn nötig, umschrieb. Er ließ eine Stimme für Violine I und Oboe I sowie eine für Violine II und Oboe II drucken. An manchen Stellen gelang es dem Notenstecher, die beiden Stimmen auf einem Liniensystem unterzubringen, aber meist ließ er einfach das aus, was ihm weniger wichtig erschien. In Nr. 9 war das Resultat verheerend. Dennoch wurden diese Stimmen (2 Hörner, Fagott, Streicher) immer wieder und in ganz Großbritannien benutzt, z. B. als Unterhaltungsmusik während der

Pausen in den Londoner Theatern. Mitunter wurden als Besonderheit Pauken verwendet, doch haben sich keine Stimmen erhalten. Merkwürdig ist, dass Walsh die schon damals sehr beliebten Menuette nicht ebenfalls veröffentlichte.

Hps: *Handel's Celebrated Water Musick compleat. Set for the Harpsichord* (1743) enthält alle Stücke in der von mir angegebenen Reihenfolge, mit Ausnahme von Nr. 9. Zu Händels Lebzeiten waren einige dieser Stücke in keiner anderen Form erhältlich. Händel hat die Nr. 9 eventuell vor 1743 herausgenommen, um das Stück anderweitig zu verwenden. Es kann aber auch sein, dass ein Kopist das Manuskript dieses Stücks beschädigt oder verloren hat.

Arn: Samuel Arnold's *Complete Works*, Ausgabe von 1788, die erste veröffentlichte Partitur.

HG: Händel-Gesellschaft, Band 47, herausgegeben von Friedrich Chrysander. Chrysander benutzte Arnolds Partitur als Vorlage, da ihm keine andere zur Verfügung stand.

The Famous Water Peice, teilweise von Wright veröffentlicht (1733), ist sicher nicht authentisch. Die „Ouvertüre" sieht aus wie eine aus dem Gedächtnis aufgeschriebene, unrechtmäßig veröffentlichte Fassung von Nr. 10D. Die Nummern 2 und 3 sind nicht als Kompositionen Händels bekannt, und Nr. 3 ist nur mit Cembalo aufführbar. Die fünf Stücke sind recht naiv für Trompete und Streicher instrumentiert. Nr. 5 ist in *Partenope* (1730) erschienen.

Quellennachweis der Manuskripte:

AUT: *GB-Lbl* Add. 30310 enthält die Nummern 10F und 11F in Händels eigenhändiger Handschrift (1715?), siehe weiter unten.

Gran: *GB-Lbl* Egerton 2946 gehört zu der Granville-Sammlung so genannter „library scores" [Bibliothekspartituren], die für Händels Freund Bernard Granville, den Bruder von Mrs Delany, kopiert worden sind. Die Sammlung blieb der Familie bis 1915 erhalten. Das sauber geschriebene Manuskript kann nicht früher als 1736 datiert werden, denn es enthält das Konzert aus dem *Alexanderfest*, aber auch nicht später als 1743, weil sich Nr. 9 unter den Stücken befindet, das aber für Hps nicht vorlag. Dieses Manuskript ist von allen Quellen die zuverlässigste.

BL: Fitzwilliam Music *GB-Cfm* MS 836 (BL 67), Cambridge, ist in der 1902 gekauften Barrett Lennard-Sammlung enthalten; vom älteren J. C. Smith oder einem seiner Mitarbeiter kopiert. Da Nr. 9 fehlt, muss das Manuskript späteren Datums als Gran sein.

Ayles: Die Manchester Public Library besitzt eine Partitur mit Stimmen, die von Smith oder seinen Mitarbeitern für Händels Librettisten Charles Jennens kopiert wurde. Jennens muss vorgehabt haben, die Händelschen Stücke aufzuführen. Seine beachtliche Sammlung von Manuskripten ging an den Earl of Aylesford. Im Jahre 1918 wurde die Aylesford-Sammlung von Newman Flower gekauft. Als Flower starb, kam sie nach Manchester. Die Partitur ist auf Blättern mit zehn Notensystemen geschrieben, sodass manchmal zu wenig Platz für die Fagottstimme vorhanden ist (wie z. B. in Nr. 13). Das Manuskript enthält weit mehr Fehler als

Gran oder BL. Da die Stimmen mit der Partitur übereinstimmen, muss der Kopist eine schlechte Quelle als Vorlage benutzt haben. Die zahlreichen Fehler werden an dieser Stelle nicht angegeben, siehe aber beispielsweise Nr. 6 (T. 52–54) und Nr. 18 (T. 15–22): Hier hat der Kopist eine eigene Bassstimme erfunden, die zum Teil mit der Bratschenstimme parallel läuft. Vielleicht war der untere Rand der vom Kopisten benutzten Vorlage abgerissen und daher die ursprüngliche Bassstimme verloren gegangen. Die Flötenstimmen wurden in die Oboenstimmen geschrieben, sodass die Oboisten sie spielen konnten. Es gibt insgesamt 14 Stimmen, die wie folgt bezeichnet wurden: „Hautboy I und II, Corno I und II, Tromba I und II, Violino Concertino I und II, Violino Ripieno I und II, Viola, Violoncello, Contra Basso, Basson". Die Reihenfolge der Stücke ist anders als in Gran, BL und Hps. Ayles enthält die Nr. 9, könnte also früher als BL und vor 1743 entstanden sein.

Man hat schon seit langem vermutet und schließlich um 1950 als sicher angenommen, dass die *Wassermusik* aus mindestens zwei Suiten zusammengesetzt ist. Chrysander hat sich jedoch dagegen ausgesprochen, obwohl es Beweise hierfür gibt. Chrysander empfahl übrigens dem British Museum, die zwei von Händel eigenhändig geschriebenen Sätze Nr. 10F und Nr. 11F zu erwerben, die er dann als ein „Concerto" veröffentlichte. Es handelt sich hier um frühere Fassungen von Nr. 10D und Nr. 11D (meine Nummerierung unterscheidet die beiden Fassungen nach ihren Tonarten). In der vorliegenden Taschenpartitur erscheinen sie zum ersten Mal an ihrem eigentli-

chen Platz, am Ende der ersten Suite.

Wir können uns nun eine Vorstellung davon machen, wie all diese Stücke aus den verschiedenen Quellen zusammengestellt wurden. Für die erste Vergnügungsfahrt auf dem Wasser (1715?) schrieb Händel eine Suite in F, und weil sie unter freiem Himmel gespielt werden sollte, verwendete er – vermutlich zum ersten Mal in England – Waldhörner. Die Instrumentalisten kamen wahrscheinlich aus Böhmen, woher auch Bach seine Hornisten bezog. Als die Lustfahrt von 1717 geplant wurde, hat sich Händel für den Gebrauch von Trompeten entschieden, weil sie von allen Instrumenten im Freien am wirkungsvollsten sind. Da nun die englischen Trompeter seiner Zeit fast immer in D spielten, mussten die neuen Stücke in dieser Tonart geschrieben werden. Er verwendete seine früher geschriebene Suite, um die verlangte Zeit ohne allzu große Anstrengung zu füllen, vielleicht aber auch, weil er darum gebeten worden war. Auf der anderen Seite lag ihm viel daran, die Trompeten zu verwenden. Er mag sich daran erinnert haben, dass in Nr. 10F die Gegensätze zwischen laut und leise sowie die Violinstimmen im Mittelteil im Freien ihre Wirkung verfehlt hatten. Er schrieb daher den ganzen Satz um, und zwar in einem kraftvollen Stil, und transponierte diesen sowie Nr. 11F nach D, damit er die Trompeten in der neuen Besetzung verwenden konnte. In der ursprünglichen Form waren die Sätze somit überflüssig geworden und Händel entfernte sie aus seinem Manuskript; sie sind jedoch durch Glück oder Zufall bis heute erhalten geblieben. Er fügte drei neue, komplett instrumentierte Stücke hinzu, und anscheinend war ihm so viel an einer großen Wirkung gelegen, dass er in der D-Dur-Suite auf jeden dynamischen Kontrast verzichtete. Alle fünf Stücke sollen ständig im Fortissimo gespielt werden.

In den Sätzen Nr. 15–19, die wiederum in einer anderen Tonart stehen (in G), treten die beiden Flötenarten in den Vordergrund. Sie sind so schwach besetzt, dass sie kaum für eine Lustfahrt auf dem Wasser bestimmt sein konnten. Höchstwahrscheinlich waren es diese Sätze, die während des Soupers des Königs in Chelsea gespielt und als „very fine Consort of Musick" [sehr schöne Musik] bezeichnet wurden. Der Preußische Gesandte hatte erwähnt, dass man beide Arten von Flöten auf dem Boot gespielt hatte. Wenn dem wirklich so war, spielten sie vermutlich zusammen mit den Oboen.

In Gran, BL und Hps stehen die Sätze in der Reihenfolge, die meiner Meinung nach aus dem Jahre 1717 stammt, und die ich auch in dieser Partitur bewahrt habe. Die Titel der verschiedenen Suiten stammen selbstverständlich vom Herausgeber:

I	Suite No. 1 in F	S. 1
II	Suite No. 2 in D	S. 67
III	Suite No. 3 in G	S. 88

Diese Reihenfolge war durchaus annehmbar für die „library scores", jedoch nicht für Jennens, der die Stücke als ein geschlossenes Werk aufführen wollte. Irgendjemand, möglicherweise sogar Händel selbst, hatte eine andere Reihenfolge erstellt, vielleicht für weitere Aufführungen anlässlich späterer Lustfahrten. Sie bestand aus einer Auswahl an Stücken aus der zweiten und dritten Suite, die kontrastreicher und effektvoller war. Ayles muss eine Partitur mit dieser Auswahl vorgelegen haben, denn dort ist die Reihenfolge der Stücke wie folgt:

Nr. 1–5, 7–8, 6, 9, 10D, 11D, 15–16, 13–14, 17–19, 12

Auch in Arn und HG wird diese Reihenfolge befolgt, nur steht dort die Nr. 6 zwischen den Nummern 5 und 7. Arnold kannte die ursprüngliche Reihenfolge, zog es aber vor, das Werk als ein geschlossenes Ganzes zu drucken.

Wer die vorliegende Taschenpartitur und die dazugehörigen Stimmen verwendet, kann selbstverständlich auch Arnolds Anordnung der Sätze befolgen oder eine eigene, beliebige Auswahl treffen. Es liegt auf der Hand, dass diese Ausgabe nicht zum Durchspielen von Anfang bis zum Ende gedacht ist, es sei denn, die Trompetensuite wird am Schluss wiederholt. Händel wiederholte sogar die beiden ersten Suiten am Ende. Bei Aufführungen dieser Art müssen die Nummern 10F und 11F ausgelassen werden. Jede Suite kann auch alleine aufgeführt werden. Die erste Suite ist in diesem Fall besonders effektvoll; oder die Hornsuite und die Trompetensuite können hintereinander gespielt werden (ohne die Nummern 10F und 11F), was dann genau der Aufführung auf der Themse im Jahre 1717 entspräche.

Anmerkungen des Herausgebers

Im Großen und Ganzen habe ich mich an Gran und BL gehalten, die beide sehr genau sind, gut übereinstimmen und meiner Meinung nach Kopien des Originalmanuskripts sind. Ayles wurde dagegen von einer weniger zuverlässigen Partitur abgeschrieben. Die ohnehin selten angegebenen Titel, Tempobezeichnungen usw. habe ich allen vorhandenen Quellen entnommen. Wenn nicht anders angegeben, sind sie in Gran und BL zu finden. Die Bezeichnung „Tempo in BL" bedeutet, dass in den anderen Quellen keine Tempobezeichnungen zu finden sind.

Es ist kaum anzunehmen, dass sich auf dem Schiff ein Cembalo befand. Händel achtete darauf, dass die Harmonisierung aller Stücke vollständig und eine Bezifferung der Bässe daher überflüssig war. Gran gibt keine Bezifferungen an, BL nur im ersten Teil von Nr. 5 und in Nr. 17. PP/Ov, PP und Ayles haben voll bezifferte Bässe, aber die Bezifferungen weisen wenig Übereinstimmungen auf; in PP sind sie außerdem sehr ungenau. Sie zu vergleichen, nähme viel Platz in Anspruch und ist nicht von so großem Interesse. Es ist höchst unwahrscheinlich, dass auch nur ein Teil der erhaltenen Bezifferungen von Händel selbst stammt. Ich habe es daher vorgezogen, sie gar nicht anzugeben. Arnolds Bezifferungen sind sinnvoll und können in HG gefunden werden.

Bei den Hornstimmen gibt es gewisse Schwierigkeiten. In Gran, BL und (größtenteils) in Ayles sind sie in der ersten Suite wie üblich geschrieben, d. h. in C notiert und ohne Vorzeichen. In der Trompetensuite bei Gran, BL und Ayles (Partitur) sind jedoch alle Blechblasinstrumente nicht transponiert angegeben und mit zwei Kreuzen versehen. Die englischen Trompetenstimmen wurden fast immer auf diese Art notiert. Auch Händel hielt sich meistens an diese Tradition. Vielleicht hat er, um Arbeit zu sparen, die Trompeten in Nr. 12 und Nr. 14 mit den Hörnern aus dem gleichen Notensystem spielen lassen. Jedenfalls sind die Stimmen in Gran und BL so geschrieben worden. Da aber Vorzeichen in Hornstimmen sehr selten vorkamen, wurde diese Schreibart vom Kopisten des Ayles-Manuskripts abgelehnt und die Hornstimmen der gesamten Trompetensuite nach C transponiert. Die Hornstimmen in PP sind transponiert. Auch ich habe diese Schreibart vorgezogen, hoffe aber, nicht inkonsequent zu erscheinen, da die Trompetenstimmen nicht transponiert und mit Vorzeichen versehen sind.

Gran und BL geben „Bassons" im Plural an, aber da die Stimme durchweg unisono bleibt, ist nicht festzustellen, ob damit zwei oder mehrere Fagotte gemeint sind.

Eckige Klammern enthalten Ergänzungen des Herausgebers. Vom Herausgeber hinzugefügte Bögen und Bindungen sind durch gestrichelte Linien gekennzeichnet.

Besetzung

I [Hornsuite]
  2 Oboen (4 Spieler?)
  1 Fagott (2 Spieler?)
  2 Hörner (4 Spieler?)
  Streicher

II [Trompetensuite]
  2 Oboen (4 Spieler?)
  1 Fagott (2 Spieler?)
  2 Hörner (4 Spieler?)
  2 Trompeten (4 Spieler?)
  Streicher

III [Flötensuite]
  2 Sopranblockflöten (ein Spieler, auch Querflöte)
  1 Fagott
  Streicher
  Cembalo

Im Jahre 1717 konnte Händel über „50 Instrumente jeglicher Art" verfügen. Die Bläserstimmen waren bestimmt doppelt besetzt und sollten, soweit möglich, auch heute verdoppelt werden.

In der Flötensuite sollten die Streicher reduziert und ein Cembalo verwendet werden. In den anderen Suiten ist das Cembalo ad libitum.

Roger Fiske (1973)
Übersetzung: Stefan de Haan

PRÉFACE

Le 19 juillet 1717, le *Daily Courant* se fit l'écho d'un évènement remontant à l'avant-veille :

« Mercredi soir, vers 8 heures, le roi s'embarqua à bord d'une barge ouverte à Whitehall [...] et se dirigera en amont vers Chelsea. Beaucoup d'autres barges occupées par des personnes de qualité l'accompagnaient [...]. Pour la musique, on avait retenu un bateau de la City Company sur lequel furent placés 50 instruments de toutes sortes qui jouèrent pendant toute la remontée depuis Lambeth (les embarcations, portées sans ramer par la marée, atteignirent Chelsea) les plus belles symphonies composées expressément pour l'occasion par Mr Hendel [*sic*], et que Sa Majesté apprécia tellement qu'il demanda qu'on les rejouât trois fois à l'aller et au retour. A onze heures, Sa Majesté accosta à Chelsea où un dîner fut servi. Il y eut alors un autre très beau concert de musique qui dura jusqu'à deux heures ; ensuite, Sa Majesté réembarqua sur la barge et reprit le chemin en sens inverse, la musique continua de jouer jusqu'à ce qu'il débarque. »

Dans un compte-rendu personnel, Friedrich Bonet, Ministre Résident prussien à Londres, ajouta que les instruments embarqués comprenaient des trompettes, des cors, des hautbois, des bassons, des flûtes allemandes, des flûtes à bec et des cordes, que chaque exécution dura une heure, qu'il y eut deux exécutions avant le dîner et une après, et que l'orchestre, qui coûta £150, fut payé par le baron Kielmansegge (l'épouse du baron, madame Kielmansegge, bien que plus âgée que lui, fut la maîtresse de George Ier).

Le premier biographe de Haendel, John Mainwaring, rapporta une anecdote concernant une fête organisée en 1715 au bord du fleuve pour laquelle Haendel aurait écrit de la musique. Bien que certains détails de son récit aient été démentis depuis, il paraît vraisemblable que de telles festivités eurent lieu avant celle de 1717 et que d'autres suivirent plus tard au cours du siècle. Dans une lettre datée du 14 juillet 1722 (citée dans son autobiographie), Mrs Delany relata une soirée au cours de laquelle des bateaux à rames, à bord desquels « le concert se composait de trois hautbois, deux bassons, une flûte allemande et la trompette du jeune Grenoc », remontèrent le fleuve de Whitehall Stairs à Richmond. Cette formation n'aurait certes pas pu jouer *Water Music* de Haendel, mais certaines pièces, qui en furent prétendument extraites, purent très bien avoir été composées et publiées pour d'autres fêtes aquatiques auxquelles Haendel ne participa en rien.

La partition autographe de *Water Music* disparut dès le XVIIIe siècle (abimée par le vent et l'humidité ?) et l'œuvre ne fut jamais convenablement publiée du vivant de Haendel, situation qui entraîna des regrets exagérés nullement justifiés de la part des éditeurs, en particulier de Chrysander. En effet, en dépit de ce qui fut affirmé, l'œuvre survécut dans des manuscrits en bon état qui concordent assez bien, entièrement orchestrée et suivant un ordre raisonné.

Les sources imprimées ne sont, en revanche, d'aucune aide et je les ai très peu utilisées. Les principales sont recensées ci-dessous par ordre chronologique. J'ai emprunté certaines informations les concernant à William C. Smith : *Handel, A Descriptive Catalogue* (Londres, 1960). Les pièces sont désignées par la numérotation adoptée dans cette édition de la partition d'étude. Les abréviations désignant les sources, et placées à leur gauche, sont employées ensuite dans l'appareil critique. PP désigne les parties imprimées (*Printed Parts*).

Arrangements de menuets. Le n° 6 et le n° 12 figurent, arrangés pour le clavecin, dans *The Lady's Banquet* III (1720, seule l'édition réalisée vers 1732 semble avoir survécu), le n° 6 sous les titres de '*Phillis the lovely*' et '*Thirsis, afflicted with Love*' (vers 1725) ainsi que dans des opéras-ballades (par exemple Air n°19 de *Polly* de Gay en 1729) ; le n°12 sous les titres de '*When I beheld Clarinda's Eyes*' et '*Hark, how the Trumpet sounds*' (vers 1720) ainsi que dans des opéras-ballades (par exemple Air 28 de *Polly* et de *Momus turn'd Fabulist*) ; le n°17 sous le titre de '*Lovely Cloe*' (vers 1725 et dans *The Musical Miscellany* V). Les menuets nos 6 et 12 sont généralement désignés comme « Menuet pour le cor (*French Horn)*» et « Menuet avec trompette » sans référence à *Water Music*. Les basses, là où elles apparaissent, ne sont pas dues à Haendel.

PP/Ov. *Six Overtures for Violins in all their Parts*, troisième recueil de Walsh, comprend l'ouverture de *Water Music* parmi des ouvertures d'opéras de Haendel. Le manuscrit de Smith indique 1725, mais les parties (incomplètes) de la source BL comprennent *Admeto* et ne peuvent donc être antérieures à 1727. L'ouverture de *Water Music* figure également dans des recueils d'ouvertures de Haendel plus tardifs et plus importants. Ces éditions se présentent toutes de la même façon. Les huit parties en sont : *Hautboy, Violino Primo, Violino Secondo, Violino Primo Ripieno, Violino Secondo Ripieno, Tenor, Bassoon e Violoncello, Basso Continuo*.

PP. *The Celebrated Water Musick in seven Parts* (1733) comprend les nos 3, 4, 8–9, 10D, 11D, 13–16 dans cet ordre, suggérant que Walsh fit sa sélection à partir d'une source suivant l'ordre que j'ai adopté, à savoir et à n'en pas douter le manuscrit autographe de 1717. Les orchestres des théâtres ou d'autres lieux disposant alors rarement de trompettes, Walsh incorpora les notes de trompette à la partie de cor, modifiant celle-ci si nécessaire. Il réalisa une partie pour le violon I et le hautbois 1, une autre pour le violon II et le hautbois 2. Le graveur réussit parfois à faire figurer les deux lignes instrumentales sur une seule portée mais, le plus souvent, il omit celle qui paraissait la moins importante. Dans le n° 9, le résultat de cette manipulation s'avère chaotique. Cette formation instrumentale (2 cors, basson, cordes) était toutefois constamment sollicitée dans toute l'Angleterre, par exemple comme entracte dans les théâtres londoniens. Il arrivait que la présence de timbales fût annoncée en attraction spéciale mais aucune partie n'en subsiste. Il semble étrange que Walsh ait laissé de côté les menuets pourtant déjà populaires.

Hps [clavecin]. *Handel's Celebrated Water Musick compleat. Set for the Harpsichord* (1743) ne contient pas le n° 9 mais toutes les autres pièces dans l'ordre que j'ai adopté. Certaines ne furent pas disponibles sous une autre forme du vivant de Haendel. En 1743, Haendel retira peut-être le n° 9 en vue de l'insérer dans une autre œuvre ou il se peut qu'il ait été égaré ou abimé par un copiste.

Arn. Edition des « Œuvres complètes » par Samuel Arnold (1788), première grande partition publiée.

HG. *Händelgesellschaft*, vol.47, édité par Friedrich Chrysander qui fonda son édition sur celle d'Arnold, seule grande partition à laquelle il eut accès.

The Famous Water Peice, publié en parties séparées par Wright (1733) est sûrement une contrefaçon. L'*Overture* ressemble à une version piratée du n°10D, transcrite de mémoire, le n° 2 et le n° 3 sont inconnus des pièces attribuées à Haendel et le n° 3 ne peut pas être joué sans clavecin. Les cinq pièces sont instrumentées de façon simpliste pour trompette et cordes. Le n° 5 parut dans *Partenope* (1730).

Les sources manuscrites :

AUT : British Library Royal Music Collection *GB-Lbl* Add.30310 contient le manuscrit autographe de Haendel du n° 10F et du n° 11F (1715 ? Voir ci-dessous).

Gran : *GB-Lbl* Egerton 2946 appartient à la collection Granville de partitions « de bibliothèque » copiées pour Bernard Granville, frère de Mrs Delany et ami de Haendel. La collection est restée dans cette famille jusqu'en 1915. Ce manuscrit soigneusement transcrit ne peut pas être antérieur à 1736 puisqu'il contient le Concerto « *Alexander's Feast* », ni postérieur à 1743 puisqu'il comprend le n° 9, qui n'est pas disponible dans la source pour clavecin (*Hps*). Cette source s'avère la plus fiable.

BL : Fitzwilliam Music *GB-Cfm* MS 836 (BL 67), conservé à Cambridge, appartient à la collection Barrett Lennard achetée en 1902. Il s'agit d'une autre copie « de bibliothèque » réalisée par J.C.Smith l'aîné ou l'un de ses assistants. Comme elle ne présente pas le n° 9, elle doit être postérieure à la source Gran.

Ayles : La Manchester Public Library possède une partition et un ensemble de parties séparées copiés par Smith ou ses assistants à l'intention du librettiste de Haendel, Charles Jennens, probablement en vue d'une exécution. L'importante collection de manuscrits de ce dernier passa au Earl of Aylesford. En 1918, la collection Aylesford fut achetée par Newman Flower, à la mort duquel elle fut léguée à Manchester. La partition est transcrite sur du papier à dix portées qui ne laissa parfois pas la place au copiste de noter la partie de basson (par exemple dans le n° 13). Cette copie présente beaucoup plus d'erreurs que les sources Gran ou BL. Les parties séparées concordant cependant avec la partition, le copiste dut s'appuyer sur une source de moins bonne qualité. Les nombreuses erreurs ne sont pas recensées ci-dessous, voir néanmoins le n° 6 (mes.52–54) et le n° 18 (mes.15–22) où le copiste arrangea sa propre basse qui double la plupart du temps l'alto. Il se peut que la portée de basse de sa source ait été déchirée au bas de la page. Les parties de flûte furent notées dans les parties de hautbois de façon à pouvoir être jouées par les hautboïstes. Les 14 parties séparées sont : *Hautboy I* et *II, Corno I* et *II, Tromba I* et *II, Violino Concertino I* et *II, Violino 'Ripieno' I* et *II, Viola, Violoncello, Contra Basso, 'Basson'*. L'ordre des pièces n'est pas le même que celui rencontré dans les sources Gran, BL et Hps. La source Ayles, qui comprend le n° 9, peut être antérieure à BL et postérieure à 1743.

On a longtemps supposé, puis admis dans les années 1950, que *Water Music* était un amalgame d'au moins deux suites, or cette idée fut rejetée par Chrysander malgré les preuves qu'il en eut. C'est lui qui conseilla au British Museum d'acheter les deux autographes de Haendel, n°10F et n°11F, et qui les publia séparément comme « concerto ». Ces mouvements sont des versions antérieures des n°s 10D et 11D (mon énumération les distingue par leurs tonalités [F= *fa*, D= *ré*]) qui sont publiées ici pour la première fois à leur juste place, à la fin de la première suite.

Il est maintenant possible d'envisager la façon dont cette musique fut rassemblée dans les diverses sources. Pour la première fête aquatique (1715 ?), Haendel écrivit une suite en *fa* destinée à être jouée en plein air et pour laquelle il eut recours, pour pratiquement la première fois en Angleterre, au cor (*French Horn*). Les cornistes venaient probablement de Bohême, comme ce fut le cas de ceux de Bach. Lorsque la fête aquatique de 1717 fut lancée, Haendel décida d'inclure des trompettes, d'un plus grand effet à l'extérieur, à la formation. Comme les trompettistes anglais jouaient généralement en *ré*, Haendel composa de nouvelles pages dans cette tonalité. Il reprit sa première suite, à la fois pour remplir le temps dévolu à la musique avec le minimum d'effort, et peut-être aussi parce qu'on le lui avait demandé, mais ne voulut pas retarder trop longtemps l'intervention des trompettes. Se souvenant peut-être de l'inefficacité, lors de l'exécution en plein air, des contrastes dynamiques du n° 10F ainsi que de l'écriture de la partie de violon dans la partie médiane, Haendel réécrivit complètement ce mouvement dans un style plus vigoureux et le transposa, ainsi que le n° 11F, en *ré* de façon à ajouter des trompettes à l'instrumentation. La version originale de ces mouvements faisant double emploi,

Haendel l'écarta du manuscrit autographe. C'est par hasard qu'elle survécut. Haendel ajouta trois pièces pour la formation complète et, avide d'éclat, ne se permit aucun contraste dynamique dans la suite en *ré* majeur : les cinq mouvements qui la composent doivent être intégralement jouées *fortissimo*.

Les mouvements n°s 15–19 empruntent encore une autre tonalité, celle de *sol*, et recourent aux deux principales formes de flûtes. Leur instrumentation délicate ne les destinant sûrement pas aux fêtes aquatiques, il paraît probable qu'ils constituèrent le « *very fine Consort of Musick* » exécuté pendant le dîner du roi à Chelsea. Le Ministre Résident prussien releva que les deux sortes de flûtes furent jouées sur le bateau. Si celles-ci furent utilisées dans les pièces jouées en plein air, elles doublèrent certainement les parties de hautbois.

Les sources Gran, BL et Hps respectent l'ordre que je pense être celui de 1717. Je l'ai maintenu ici. Les intitulés des suites ont été, bien sûr, ajoutés à l'édition :

I   Suite n° 1 en *fa*   p.1
II Suite n° 2 en *ré*   p.67
III Suite n° 3 en *sol* p.88

Cet ordre convenait aux manuscrits « de bibliothèque », mais pas à Jennens qui désirait exécuter cette musique en une œuvre unique. Une autre intervention, peut-être de Haendel lui-même en vue d'autres fêtes aquatiques, établit une ordre des différents mouvements qui mélangeait la deuxième et la troisième suites de manière à augmenter les contrastes et à obtenir un final éclatant. La source Ayles procède d'une telle partition et présente les mouvements ainsi :

1–5, 7–8, 6, 9, 10D, 11D, 15–16, 13–14, 17–19, 12

Les sources Arn et HG respectèrent cet

ordre, à l'exception du n° 6 placé entre les n°s 5 et 7. Arnold connaissait l'ordre original mais préféra imprimer l'œuvre comme un ensemble unique. Rien n'empêche d'utiliser cette partition et ses parties séparées en adoptant l'ordre d'Arnold ou tout autre ordre personnel. Cette édition ne doit, à l'évidence, pas être jouée intégralement à moins de reprendre la Suite avec trompettes à la fin. Haendel reprenait les *deux* premières suites à la fin. Lors de telles exécutions, on retirera le n° 10F et le n° 11F. Chacune des suites peut être jouée seule, la première produisant, dans ce cas, le meilleur effet. La Suite avec cors et la Suite avec trompettes peuvent être jouées l'une après l'autre (sans le n° 10F ni le n°11F), ainsi qu'elles le furent sur la Tamise en 1717.

Appareil critique

J'ai, en général, suivi les sources Gran et BL, très précises et très similaires. Je les crois copiées à partir du manuscrit autographe, tandis que la source Ayles fut copiée à partir d'une source moins fiable. J'ai reproduit les titres, les indications de tempo, etc., rencontrés dans toutes les sources tant ces détails sont peu nombreux. Si elles ne sont pas mentionnées ci-dessous, ces indications se trouvent dans les sources Gran et BL. « *Tempo in BL* » signifie que cette indication ne figure dans aucune autre source.

Un clavecin n'ayant pas pu être embarqué, Haendel s'assura que l'harmonie de l'œuvre était complète et n'eut aucune raison de chiffrer la basse. La source Gran ne présente aucun chiffrage, la source BL en indique dans la première partie du n° 5 et dans le n° 17. Les sources PP/Ov, PP et Ayles sont entièrement chiffrées mais ces chiffrages divergent, ceux de PP étant extrêmement inexacts. Etablir une concordance entre les chiffrages serait de peu d'intérêt et prendrait beaucoup de place. Il est tellement improbable qu'aucun des chiffrages

existant soit de Haendel que j'ai préféré ne pas en donner du tout. Les chiffrages d'Arnold s'avèrent néanmoins justes et figurent dans la source HG.

Les parties de cor posent un problème. Dans la Suite n° 1, les sources Gran, BL et (en grande partie) Ayles les présentent de la manière habituelle, à savoir en *ut* sans armure de tonalité, tandis que dans la Suite avec trompettes, Gran, BL et Ayles (grande partition) présentent toutes les parties de cuivre *loco* avec deux dièses à la clef. Les parties de trompettes anglaises étaient presque toujours transcrites de cette façon et le furent également par Haendel. Dans les n°s 12 et 14, Haendel s'est sûrement simplifié la tâche en faisant doubler les trompettes par les cors notés sur la même portée, ainsi que ces parties figurent dans les sources Gran et BL. Cependant, les armures de tonalités étaient alors tout-à-fait inhabituelles pour les parties de cor et le copiste de la source Ayles les rejeta et transposa en *ut* les parties de cor de toute la Suite avec trompettes. La source PP présente des parties de cor transpositeur et j'ai privilégié cette convention, en espérant qu'il ne paraît pas incohérent de laisser les parties de trompette *loco* avec une armure de tonalité.

L'orthographe de « Bassons » au pluriel est commune aux sources Gran et BL bien que cette partie ne soit jamais divisée et que le recours à deux bassons ou plus demeure incertain.

Indications éditoriales : les ajouts éditoriaux sont placés entre crochets [ ], les liaisons de phrasé ou les liaisons de notes complétées par l'éditeur sont indiquées en pointillée ⌐⁻⁻⁻⌐.

Instrumentation

I. [Suite avec cors]
2 hautbois (4 instrumentistes ?)
1 basson (2 instrumentistes)
2 cors (4 instrumentistes ?)
cordes

II. [Suite avec trompettes]
2 hautbois (4 instrumentistes ?)
1 basson (2 instrumentistes ?)
2 cors (4 instrumentistes ?)
2 trompettes (4 instrumentistes ?)
cordes

III. [Suite avec flûtes]
2 flûtes à bec soprano (l'une dou-
blant la flûte traversière)
1 basson
cordes
clavecin

En 1717, Haendel disposait de « 50 instruments de toutes sortes ». Les parties des instruments à vent étaient certainement doublées et devraient, si possible, toujours l'être.

Dans la Suite avec flûtes, on réduira le nombre de cordes et on ajoutera un clavecin. Dans les autres suites, le recours au clavecin est facultatif.

Roger Fiske
(1973)
Traduction : Agnès Ausseur

WATER MUSIC

George Frideric Handel
(1685–1759)

Suite No. 1 in F
HWV 348

1. Ouverture

Edited by Roger Fiske
© 1973 Ernst Eulenburg Ltd
and Ernst Eulenburg & Co GmbH

2

4

6

8

10

Alternative ending

[Repeat from bar 14]

12

2. **Adagio e staccato**

14

16

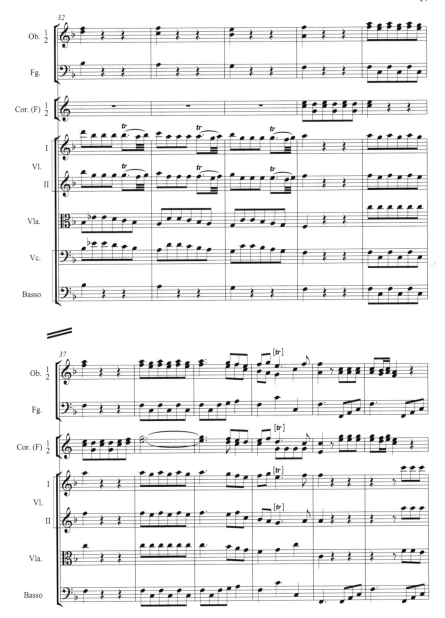

24

[Fine]

Da Capo

4. **Presto**

30

[*Fine*]

Da Capo

5. Air

Presto

6. Minuet for the French Horn

36

[Fine]

38

Da Capo

7. Bourrée

'3 times, 1st all the Violins, 2nd all the Hautboys, 3rd all together' *

Presto

* 'Violins' means all the strings; 'Hautboys' includes bassoons

40

8. Hornpipe
'3 times in the same manner'

9.

44

EE 7105

46

EE 7105

47

EE 7105

48

10 F.

51

52

53

EE 7105

54

57

Dal Segno

58

11 F.

Alla Hornpipe

60

61

64

65

EE 7105

66

Da Capo

Suite No. 2 in D
HWV 349

10 D.

68

Adagio

11 D.

76

[*Fine*]

[*Da Capo*]

82

12. Trumpet Minuet

'3 times, 1st Trumpets & Violins; 2nd Horns & Hautboys; 3rd all together'*

* 'Violins' means all the strings; 'Hautboys' includes bassoons

84

13.

Lentement

[*Fine*]

Da Capo

14.
'This Aire is to be play'd thrice' *

* The instrumentation should vary as in No. 12

Suite No. 3 in G
HWV 350

15.

16.

Presto

* The Violino I stave may be played by a Flauto traverso

[Fine]

[Da Capo]

17. Menuet

94

18.

* Descant Recorders sounding an octave higher

Da Capo

19. Country Dance